Fragments of Her

Kacie Ketch

Fragments of Her © 2022 Kacie Ketch

All rights reserved.

No part of this publication may be reproduced, stored in a retrieval system, or transmitted, in any form or by any means, electronic, mechanical, photocopying, recording or otherwise, without the prior written permission of the presenters.

Kacie Ketch asserts the moral right to be identified as author of this work.

Presentation by *BookLeaf Publishing*

Web: www.bookleafpub.com

E-mail: info@bookleafpub.com

ISBN: 9789357613385

First edition 2022

DEDICATION

To my moon, Jesse. You are the light in my darkest moments.

Time

Time's rose coloured lips
press gently on mine
she is my cruel mistress
ticking away hours and days
but as the wise women say
she also heals wounds
and reveals all things

I stare into Time's golden eyes
they meet mine with satisfaction
that she has done a job well done
she has caressed my face
held my hands in hers
and left her gentle mark
that she has passed
and will continue to pass

I run her dark hair through my fingers
it is soft and tangible
and yet so obscure
she is clear as day in front of me
yet so vague

We sit together over a cup of tea
reminiscing
chatting about past lovers

past lives
past selves
and before I know it
my tea has gone cold
I take a sip and yet
I am surprised
despite Time sitting with me
the whole time

I watch a smile curl across
Time's lips
her teeth shine like moonlight
she laughs at me
and my foolishness
to forget her
even for a moment
because despite what wise women say
Time is still my cruel mistress
and she waits for no man.

Vestiges & Remains

Even after the sun sets
I can still feel her warmth on my skin
and carry the freckles she bestowed upon me

The night comes
and with it the vestiges of our
celestial fire
the remnants of the day
and the remains of sunshine
ice melted
flowers bloomed
children with sun tans
and ice cream stains

But what will I leave behind
when my day is done?
will I leave reminders on
the skin of my sons
of just how much their mother loves them?
when the night comes
will they cower in darkness
or remember that the sun always rises again?
will I make the flowers in them bloom?

My only wish is

that my remnants do not
haunt them
leave them chasing ghosts
or what ifs
be at peace
because just like the sun
I will always return
and when the night falls
my vestiges will remain with you.

I Think I Own the Sky Now

I think I own the sky now
her dark nights
lacking of stars or northern lights
belong to my sadness and emptiness
but her sunshine
and ocean blue skies
they belong to the days
I feel I can conquer the world

maybe one day I'll own that too

The purple and pink paradise
of sunset
worship me and whisk me off to bed
her starry night
fills my head with dreams
of art and poetry

How could she not be mine?
every day she awakens the sun for me
every night the moon waits
for me in my bed
so that he may carry me to sleep

I watch her bring me shooting stars

so that I may make
wishes upon them
or love under them

You may think me bold
or arrogant
for calling the sky we share mine
but she is my most consistent friend
and devoted lover

Who else has painted a new
horizon for me each day
or listened to each of my cries
or when I've howled at the moon?

I think I own the sky now
in the way a silhouetted tree
owns the sunset
or the moon owns the night

It is divine
and destiny
that life's only consistency
should be mine.

Ghost Town

Street lights illuminate empty store fronts
sidewalks chattering
reminiscing of the day's travels
upper-level apartment windows
with blinds closed tight
all the life contained
in lifeless buildings

Traffic lights become obsolete
stopping cars
waving people through
that are elsewhere

Quarter past midnight
and you forget
how your lips became bitter with alcohol

Walking through empty streets
dark houses wave goodbye as you pass
the wind kisses you goodnight
wisps you off your feet
you feel like a child again
when your parents would still carry you to bed
now you're grown
and instead he's the one

who carries you

He pours you a drink
and another
and another
and your pour yourself onto his lap

You leave the streetlights on so
he can see to cross the street
hear the echo of the emptiness
and your legs chatter
reminiscing of past lovers

Time to open the blinds
reveal what's behind the curtain
but you forget where it went
because you are the ghost town.

Falling Rain

The rain refuses to leave the cloud
like a child holding his mother
on the first day of school
you believe the dark skies
linger and taunt
but I know they are just shy
timid even
lacking the courage
to create a thunderous storm
or to make you dance in the rain

Do not be that rain-filled cloud
apprehensive and faint-hearted
summon your courage
and take the world by storm
or go rejoice under the crackling sky

Grey clouds rarely seize the day.

Sun & Moon

I am in love with the moon
and the way he quietly sings me
to sleep each night
his beams shine through my window
and caress my body
he whispers softly to me
while he calms the wolf within me
that howls into the darkness

I love the moon
and how his face changes
each night

But I love the sun too
her celestial fire brings new life
sweetens the earth beneath me
makes flowers bloom where
I thought they could not

But you'll ask me
"How can you love the sun
when you have never felt her warmth
on your skin?"
and you'd be right
I've never touched the sun

or felt her burn after
a day of worship

I have not called the sun mine
but it does not make me
love her any less
I watch her rise each day
turning black skies blue
and banishing away stars
until the day's end

I love my moon
but I love the sun as well
in the ways they are different
and the same
the duality of my love
is what defines me
not who's touched my skin
or who lays with me
at the end of each day

My love is as ever changing
as the sky
and with each night's moon
and every rising sun
I will love some more.

Slow-Motion Suicide

I light a cigarette
and another
and another
I can't remember
my last unadulterated breath
or the last time I felt this alive

To hold death between two fingers
billowing smoke and red ember
but to just as easily crush death
in a dirty ashtray
filled with the death of strangers prior

But what is death if not instant
and what is suicide if not
inviting the very thing that kills you
between your lips

I inhale
and feel my death in slow-motion
my lungs collapse on themselves
and my heart pumps the poison through me

I feel another day pass
or year

or whatever it is they say
but not today
maybe tomorrow
or the next day
but not today

Instead I'll feel the slow burn of smoke
and the slow death from this cigarette.

Vessel

When I finally lay to rest
take my body
leave my soul

Take the steps I walked
but leave behind the mountains I conquered
take the bumps and lumps
leave the love
the kindness

Take the hills and valleys
the counting and dieting
the self-hate
but leave the pieces of me that battled
the parts of me that sometimes lost
and picked myself up afterwards

Take my body
the too-tall awkward teenager
the fat friend who would have given anything
to cut away pieces of herself
the woman who made herself small

But please leave my soul
leave the safe haven and listening ear

leave the girl whose power lived in her voice
leave the person I became:
the mother, partner, friend
an advocate, a fighter

Take my body
leave my soul
take the curves and rolls
and the prejudices that came with them
take the trauma and scars and heartache

and leave what's left

Take away the vessel
and keep me with you.

Undressed

Undressed
after waiting for him in a dimly lit room
he tosses my clothes on the floor
and my heart

Undressed
a goodnight kiss is what he asks for
but he gasps for one last breath
and my lips are like air
I get drunk on the night's promise
on his tongue
but he never keeps his promises

Undressed
"please don't leave me, please don't hurt me"
and he whispers back
"I never will"
I lay on his chest
mine has been cut open
so I let him reach his hand in and hold me close

Undressed
I'm back in that dimly lit room
he tosses my clothes on the floor
and my heart

I wonder if he'll ever pick it up.

leave the girl whose power lived in her voice
leave the person I became:
the mother, partner, friend
an advocate, a fighter

Take my body
leave my soul
take the curves and rolls
and the prejudices that came with them
take the trauma and scars and heartache

and leave what's left

Take away the vessel
and keep me with you.

Undressed

Undressed
after waiting for him in a dimly lit room
he tosses my clothes on the floor
and my heart

Undressed
a goodnight kiss is what he asks for
but he gasps for one last breath
and my lips are like air
I get drunk on the night's promise
on his tongue
but he never keeps his promises

Undressed
"please don't leave me, please don't hurt me"
and he whispers back
"I never will"
I lay on his chest
mine has been cut open
so I let him reach his hand in and hold me close

Undressed
I'm back in that dimly lit room
he tosses my clothes on the floor
and my heart

I wonder if he'll ever pick it up.

What Was Not Seen But Heard

I am awakened
far off sounds echo through my room
as I lay listening to the soft blasts

A heavy mist has fallen on the town
there is nothing but fog outside
houses and parked cars have vanished
into not-so-thin air
and all that's left
are the sounds of the night
and those three soft horns

quiet for a moment
and then three more

You move silently across the river
except for your three soft horns

What peace
and terror you must feel
to move across the water
with no horizon
no view
just fog

Your horns grow quieter
as you continue your journey
my eyes grow heavier
with each fading blast
and the mist carries me off to sleep
once again.

A Poem To My White Mother

Your blue eyes
deep as an ocean
cast their gaze upon mine
reflections of generations past
dance
and cry out
their light eyes
disappeared
their fair skin
lost to the Middle East

Our family photos
still hang on your walls
beautiful blonde haired babies
surround and over take me
I see my disappearance
and simultaneous spotlight
from the family around me
who hardly look like family at all

Your culture became mine
my heritage left behind
in the Persian Gulf
celebrations of Nowruz

dinners of tahdig and dried fruit
an entire language lost

Because you can't teach
what you don't know
and you never knew Iran.

The Sin of Woman

Sinner from birth
repenting for a body
she did not choose
her skin is home to shame
taught to her by men
who lust after her innocence
her value is synonymous with her virtue
her worth measured from the pursuit of being
pure

Man serves the lord
and she must serve man
he kneels in prayer
and she kneels to him
starving herself in the name of beauty
while he feasts
on the fruits of her labour

A vessel for his pleasure
but she's the one paying
for transgressions they both commit

"Forgive me Father for I have sinned,"
the sweetness on her breath from an apple
she did not bite

you'd call her a temptress
a whore
when she did nothing more
than be born a daughter
and not a son.

A Letter Never Delivered

I sign my name
and seal the envelope
with all the things I wish
I'd had the time to say

The letter is addressed
but I know it will never reach you
the house number the same
the street name unchanged
just no longer yours

I filled my pen with tears fallen
in hopes you will receive
just how much I miss you

Your number is still saved in my phone
but who now will answer?
how I wish I could call you
just to tell you about my day
or remind you how loved you are

But I know you cannot answer the phone
and I know my letter will never be delivered.

He Is

He is the sun that shines
through my window
beams through the pane
illuminating my world
turning even dust
into glitter

He is the storm on a sweltering day
and the rain soaked through to my skin
his voice thunderous and
his eyes piercing like lightning
straight through me
sending shockwaves to my very core
he is electric
makes my hairs stand on end
my heart palpitate

But like the sun and the rain
he is not infinite
there will come a day
when dusk will fall over me
and he will send me off with
pink and orange skies
that will sing us both to sleep
the storm will end and with it

the cool rain
and the electrical current that runs
through me when he is near

He is not infinite
but I'm learning that is what
makes a thing beautiful
that it is finite
our numbered days are that much more
because they will end
one day
someday

But until then
he is warm like sunshine
and cool like a storm
he fills my days with beauty and electricity
and maybe even a little insanity
because I know what he is
and he is mine.

Torrance

Meet me where the blue house sits
by the railway tracks
where the maple tree canopies fill the sky
and the songbirds sing hello

Go to where bare feet walk on gravel down a
winding road
so that you may wash away your sins
at the end of a dock

Find that old white church
or the general store at the top of the hill
where kids eat penny candies
hoping it's not time to go home

Show me the river we caught frogs in
or childhood naïvety
so that I may find it again

Meet me where the rhubarb grows
or by the bus stop at the end of our road
and I'll show you the ice rink I fell on every year

Go to where the milkweed blooms
and find where I left that small piece of myself

so that it may have the chance to grow

I'll show you where it all began
where the hallways lead
or the stairwell guides you
and you will see the still air in this old house
and the way the dust settled on me

Go to each place I sat alone
praying the Earth would swallow me whole
or that the waves might wash me away
and I will show you where I stood again
and walked away more resilient

Find me lying in the grass outside my childhood home
watching the world turn and the sky change
just as I have changed

Meet me in this place that has been forgotten
and only now exists
through the eyes of a child that is no more
peering through a looking glass of memories

Meet me there so we may share our last communion
and show me how to close the door on this old house
so that I may leave its ghosts inside.

Things I Sometimes Know To Be True

The moon so distinctly belonging
to the night
to the stars and the darkness
but sometimes
in the light of day
you can see the moon hanging there
resting in the pale blue sky
floating like a balloon lost from
a small child's grasp

The ocean pictured kissing
the edge of a sandy shore
or lapping
over rocks at the foot of a cliff
yet here it is
echoing in the depth of your chest
waves spilling onto your tongue
sounds like the old shell
perched on the back of the toilet
in your great-aunt's bathroom

The trees swaying
back and forth in the breeze
like your best friend's hair

on a warm day in the summer
rocking back and forth
in the wind
or her head in your lap
after she's had too much to drink

And finally
the stars decorating the night sky
completing
the infinity of the universe
falling for naïve wishful thinking
they're speckled across your
little sister's cheeks
and onto her nose
and looking into his eyes
you'll never need a rocket ship
because you're already fully immersed
in the galaxy.

A Silent Understanding

A silent understanding
is only realized by strangers

Two people on the subway
meet eyes after
they both watch someone slip
on the platform
they chuckle to themselves
and then with each other
they quietly ride together
10 feet part
until one of them gets off the train
never to be seen again
this moment has been shared between them

You walk outside to light your cigarette
the cold wind chills you through
you see a man standing mere feet away
his shoulders hunched from the cold
you share a look
your minds meet somewhere between
fallen ashes
to understand how another feels
without ever standing in their shoes
is both a blessing and a curse

It's 5 o'clock
you're headed home
after another long day
another week
you see the same cars
you always do
you're all headed to the same place
and at the same time
going in entirely different directions
you begin to know people
you're never met
or even seen

To share a moment
on the subway
over a cigarette
at a red light
with a complete stranger
who will maybe one day
write a poem about you too

That is a silent understanding.

Home

I always thought when I found a home
it would have four brick walls
an old fireplace in the living room
and a chandelier
hanging above an antique wood table
where we would eat every night
the house would smell like lemons and old
books
and flowers from my garden
long lace curtains on every window
blowing in the summer breeze
and turning away the winter cold

But how could it be?

Home is not contained
it's in all the days spent laughing
driving down spiraling roads that go nowhere
and everywhere
in my mother's perfume
and the fragile grasp of my grandmother's hands
in all the words I've spilled on paper
the paint I've washed off my hands
in the empty streets I walk
when I'm drunk on the night's promise

and that last shot of tequila

Home
how could it be anything less
than a smile from a stranger on the subway
or a cup of tea
with two scoops of sugar
and a little bit of milk

Home is
letting my kid brother beat me at cards
it's in the fingertips of my lover
and diving into the lake on a hot day

I always thought when I found a home
it would have four brick walls
and an old fireplace
but home is not a place you build
so I'm realizing that home was with me
all along.

The Power of Water

There is a power to water:
it sustains you
energizes you
after a hot summer day
is there anything more divine
more holy
than a cool lake
and the relief it holds

There is a triumph to water:
a cold glass
or wet cloth
after labouring in the sun
it refreshes you
wipes away the sweat
and the heat
from a day of hard work

There is a grace to water
and mercy:
a hot shower soothes you
makes you new
and is there any purer place to suffer
than in the bottom of a bathtub

There is life to water:
rainfall extinguishes the blaze
and seeps into the Earth
creating vitality
from death

Is there anything more pure
or honest
than the thing that can
quench you
revive you
cleanse you
wash away your sins
being the very thing that
will pull you into the deep.

Sapphires & Sunflowers

Where your eyes once
sparkled like sapphires
now they are sealed with gold coins
skin stained with paint and sunflowers
and warmth and sunshine
now feeds new creation of life

Even when I knew it was
the last time
I feel robbed of a goodbye
an embrace from a deathbed
will never be as good
as one after being apart

I know you are with me
your spirit brings sunflowers into my day
fills my children's eyes with sapphires
and my heart with the memory
of a loving grandmother.

Printed in the USA
CPSIA information can be obtained
at www.ICGtesting.com
LVHW010743140324
774444LV00002B/365